TWELVE SMALL WINDOWS

TWELVE SMALL WINDOWS
Short Poems for Seeing Clearly

by J. A. Gucci
Student Edition

Pressure System Press

New York, New York

2026

TWELVE SMALL WINDOWS (Student Edition)
© 2026 J. A. Gucci
All rights reserved.

No part of this publication may be reproduced, stored in a retrieval system, or transmitted in any form or by any means — electronic, mechanical, photocopying, recording, or otherwise — without the prior written permission of the publisher, except in the case of brief quotations used for review or educational purposes.

Published by Pressure System Press
Brooklyn, New York

ISBN: 979-8-9946751-4-4

Printed in the United States of America

First Edition, 2026

www.jagucci.com

Dedication

For the ones
who stop to look
and keep looking.

Contents

Oxbow Lake 13
Frost Heave 14
The Silent Train 15
Re-calibration 16
Experience 17
Projection 18
Flicker 19
Leather Foot 20
Resilience 21
Messy Cycle 22
Ship of Theseus 23
Again, Moon 24

Author's Note

I didn't grow up surrounded by poetry.
What I did have was curiosity — and the habit of noticing strange things.

These poems aren't about imagination. They're about real phenomena: a river curling out of its path, a cuttlefish flickering in its sleep, a moon broken by ripples. You could research every image in this book and find it's not metaphor — it's matter.

Each poem is short. They don't explain. But they reward the reader who asks, "Why that detail? Why that word?"

I believe in poetry that doesn't hide, but compresses.
Poetry that doesn't invent, but observes.
Poetry that sharpens how we see.

— J. A. Gucci
2026

To the Reader

These poems are short — on purpose.

Each one shows a real thing in the world. No metaphors, no symbols. Just careful observation.

The poems are grouped around paradoxes — ideas that seem to contradict themselves, but still feel true. You'll notice each poem follows a kind of loop: change, return, or break.

You don't need to understand everything. You don't need to write like this either.

Just look closely. Read slowly. Try writing a few of your own.

If something feels strange, it means you're paying attention.

Oxbow Lake

Sun,
snow,
a mountain—
dripping,

streams rippling,
river chipping,
a bank breaks—

a lily blooms.

Frost Heave

Afternoon rain—
seeping,

dusk—
frozen water
swelling,

alligator cracking—
pothole.

The Silent Train

Ditch light—
loom—
billows and swirls,

low hum—
screeching steel on steel—
a shifting shaking ground—

a quiet roar,
footsteps on stairs.

Re-calibration

Starlings soaring through sky—
a tear drop.

Gust of wind—
a juvenile
astride,
astray—

adrift…

Experience

Hot stove:
red glow,
shimmering air,

shiny bubbles pop—
crust-dried,
smooth hands.

Hot stove:
red glow—
oven mitts.

Projection

Zenith—
gleaming—
my tiny shadow
under feet.

Level,
pale—
my long shadow
on the wall.

Flicker

A crimson cuttlefish,
asleep—
dreaming:

salmon skin—
yellow,
now green,
blue.

A blink—
crimson cuttlefish—
awake.

Leather Foot

Ant on rye—
streaking to nest—
long and windy.

Leather foot over sidewalk—
a scout scurries astray,

streaking to nest—
short and straight.

Resilience

Milk eyes,
undulating snout—

a sock—
inside out.

Dead skin—
glistening.

Messy Cycle

Rain—

sickly bruised
charcoal gray,

streaks of oil,
trapped gases,

swampy olive patches,
rotting wood—

Sacred Lotus.

Ship of Theseus

Bare branches—
snap,

sap—
frozen,
welling—

shivering wax bulbs
wobbling—
neon chartreuse,

engorged leaves,
bursting.

Dew—
sweet astringent air.

Again, Moon

Glimmering
glass lake,

a stone—
ripples—

shivering moon.

About the Paradox Triads

Each poem in this book is built on a paradox triad.

A paradox triad is a set of three words that seem to contradict each other — but when placed together, they show us how real things change, break, repeat, or return.

You'll see these triads quietly running through each poem. They don't appear in the titles or lines, but they shape how the poem moves. Like gravity, the triad pulls everything toward it.

Triads are about structure, not symbols. They help young poets think more clearly, not more abstractly. They're like tools — invisible, but reliable.

The Paradox Triads

Oxbow Lake — Start / Middle / Gone

Frost Heave — Crack / Ice / Water

The Silent Train — Noise / Echo / Silence

Re-calibration — Flock / One / Lost

Experience — Mistake / Pattern / Memory

Projection — Shadow / Shape / Sun

Flicker — Real / Dream / Wake

Leather Foot — Map / Path / Lost

Resilience — Hold / Drop / Change

Messy Cycle — Rain / Mud / Bloom

Ship of Theseus — Gone / Back / Different

Again, Moon — Same / Again / Strange

The Twelve Series

Each book in this series presents systems through short, structured poems.

Rather than describing events, the poems model how systems form, interact, and change over time.

Each volume focuses on a different civilization, using the same method to reveal how complex societies develop.

History

Mesopotamia — Formation
Greece — Interaction
Rome — Expansion and Collapse
Medieval — Thresholds

Creative Writing

Twelve Loops
Twelve Mirrors
Twelve Rooms

Philosophy

Twelve Iron Paradoxes

About the Author

J. A. Gucci is a poet, composer, and educator. He has written over a dozen books exploring how form, observation, and contradiction shape meaning.

He believes poetry doesn't need metaphor to be powerful — just attention, precision, and patience.

He has taught composition and creative process to students from elementary school to university, and continues to explore how thinking clearly and looking closely can change how we create.

This is his first book written especially for middle school readers.

www.ingramcontent.com/pod-product-compliance
Lightning Source LLC
LaVergne TN
LVHW041644070526
838199LV00053B/3549